HEAVENLY HEMP

HEAVENLY HEMP

Astrological Paths to Plant Power

MATTHEW PETCHINSKY

Apophis Enterprises LLC

CHAPTER 1

Heavenly Hemp: Astrological Paths to Plant Power
By: Matthew Petchinsky

PREFACE

Introduction to the Intertwining of Hemp and Astrology

At the heart of this book lies a profound connection between two seemingly disparate realms: the ancient plant hemp and the celestial art of astrology. This connection is not merely coincidental or superficial; it is deeply rooted in historical, cultural, and spiritual practices that span across centuries and civilizations. Hemp, with its versatile applications and misunderstood nature, mirrors the complexity and depth of astrology, a guide to understanding the cosmic influences that shape our lives and the world around us.

The intertwining of hemp and astrology opens up a unique pathway for exploring plant power and celestial wisdom. Hemp, known for its resilience and versatility, has been cultivated by humans for thousands of years, serving as a source of food, fiber, and medicine. Astrology, on the other hand, offers insights into the human condition, our relationship with the cosmos, and the subtle energies that influence us daily. By exploring the synergies between these two fields, this book aims to illuminate the ways in which the movements of celestial bodies can influence plant growth and healing properties, and how hemp can enhance our understanding and practice of astrology.

How to Navigate and Utilize the Book for Personal Growth and Understanding

This book is structured to guide you through the multifaceted relationship between hemp and astrology, from historical backgrounds and scientific insights to spiritual practices and practical applications. Whether you are new to these subjects or have some familiarity with them, the book is designed to provide a comprehensive overview while also offering deep dives into specific topics of interest.

To get the most out of this book, I encourage you to approach it with an open mind and a willingness to explore the connections between the celestial and the terrestrial. Each chapter builds upon the last, weaving a narrative that spans from the macrocosm of the cosmos to the microcosm of a hemp seed. However, feel free to navigate the chapters in a way that best suits your interests and needs.

For those seeking practical advice, the later chapters offer guidance on cultivating hemp in harmony with astrological cycles, creating personalized hemp-infused products, and integrating hemp and astrology into daily life. For readers more interested in the historical and cultural aspects, the initial chapters provide a rich context for understanding the deep roots of the connection between hemp and astrology.

Throughout the book, you will find personal reflections, case studies, and exercises designed to enhance your understanding and personal practice. These elements are intended to encourage you to explore your own relationship with hemp and astrology, fostering personal growth, healing, and a deeper connection with the natural world.

As you embark on this journey, remember that the goal is not only to acquire knowledge but also to awaken a sense of wonder and possibility. May this book serve as a guide, a companion, and an inspiration as you explore the heavenly hemp pathway and discover the astrological paths to plant power.

If you want to see some amazing products, please visit my Virtual Dispensary: https://shift.store/sg1fan23477/retail

<u>Chapter 1: Historical and Cultural Foundations</u>

The Ancient Tapestry of Hemp: Exploring Hemp's Ancient Uses, Its Journey Through Controversies, and Modern Resurgence

Hemp's journey through human history is as rich and complex as the fibers of the plant itself. Cultivated for more than 10,000 years, hemp has been an integral part of human civilization, serving myriad uses that span from textiles to medicine. Its story begins in ancient China, where it was revered for its durability and versatility. The Chinese not only used hemp to make the world's first paper but also discovered its medicinal properties, incorporating it into their traditional healing practices.

As civilizations evolved, hemp spread across the globe, finding its place in the cultures and economies of ancient India, Egypt, Persia, and eventually Europe. In each of these cultures, hemp was more than just a crop; it was a vital resource that contributed to the societal and economic development. It was used to make clothing, ropes, sails, and even as a form of currency in some regions. The plant's universality underscored its importance to ancient societies, transcending geographical and cultural boundaries.

However, hemp's journey was not without its controversies. The 20th century marked a turning point, as political, economic, and social factors led to the demonization and eventual prohibition of hemp in many parts of the world. The conflation of hemp with its psychoactive cousin, marijuana, contributed to its decline. This period saw hemp being sidelined, its potential forgotten or ignored due to the growing stigma around cannabis.

Despite these challenges, the late 20th and early 21st centuries have witnessed a resurgence of interest in hemp. This revival is driven by a greater understanding of the plant's ecological benefits, such as its minimal water requirements and its ability to replenish soil nutrients. Additionally, the rediscovery of hemp's potential in producing sustainable alternatives to plastics, fuels, and textiles has contributed to its modern renaissance. Today, as legal barriers begin to fall, hemp is reclaiming its place in the global economy and consciousness, heralding a new era of industrial and therapeutic uses.

Astrology Through the Ages: Tracing the Origins, Evolution, and the Role of Astrology in Agriculture and Herbalism

Astrology's origins are as celestial as the subject matter it studies. Rooted in the ancient world, astrology was born from humanity's observation of the stars and their cycles. The Babylonians, around the 2nd millennium BC, are credited with forming the first organized system of astrology. They developed the zodiac, a celestial coordinate system that divides the sky into twelve parts, each named after the constellation that occupies the sector. This system laid the groundwork for Western astrology, which would later be refined by the Greeks and Romans.

The role of astrology in agriculture and herbalism cannot be overstated. Ancient farmers relied on astrological calendars to guide their planting and harvesting cycles, a practice known as planting by the Moon. The phases of the Moon were believed to affect the moisture content in the soil, influencing the growth of plants. This ancient wisdom was not merely superstition but an early form of biodynamics, a holistic understanding of agricultural processes as interconnected with cosmic forces.

In herbalism, astrology provided a framework for understanding the medicinal properties of plants. Each plant was associated with a particular planet or zodiac sign, believed to influence its healing properties. This astrological botany formed the basis of many traditional healing systems, where the timing of harvesting herbs was carefully aligned with celestial events to maximize their potency.

Over the centuries, astrology has evolved, shaped by the cultures that practiced it. Despite being marginalized by the scientific revolution, astrology has endured, experiencing a resurgence in popular culture. Its principles continue to influence holistic health practices, including modern herbalism, where the ancient connections between plants and planets are being rediscovered and embraced.

Astrology's enduring presence underscores a deep-seated human desire to find meaning in the cosmos, to understand our place within a larger universe. The revival of astrological agriculture and herbalism speaks to a growing recognition of the wisdom of ancient practices, a reawakening to the interconnectedness of all life, guided by the stars above.

Through the tapestry of hemp's history and the celestial journey of astrology, Chapter 1 lays the foundation for understanding the deep connections between the earth and the cosmos. As we delve deeper into the book, these connections will be explored further, revealing the ways in which they can enrich our lives and our understanding of the world around us.

The Ancient Tapestry of Hemp: Exploring Hemp's Ancient Uses, Its Journey Through Controversies, and Modern Resurgence

The story of hemp is a journey through time, one that mirrors the evolution of human society itself. This journey begins in ancient China, around 8,000 BC, where hemp was first cultivated. The Chinese utilized hemp for a multitude of purposes, from creating the world's earliest known woven fabrics to producing paper. Hemp seeds were valued for their nutritional content, and the plant's fibers were transformed into ropes, textiles, and even building materials. This early use of hemp highlights its integral role in the development of human civilization, providing essential goods that facilitated advancements in communication, nutrition, and technology.

As trade routes expanded, so did the knowledge and use of hemp, spreading to ancient India, Mesopotamia, Egypt, and beyond. In each civilization, hemp found its place, revered for its strength, versatility, and ease of cultivation. The Egyptians used hemp to create fine linens and to treat pain and inflammation. Meanwhile, in Medieval Europe, hemp became the material of choice for sails, ropes, and clothing, underscoring the plant's importance in exploration and trade.

However, the 20th century brought about significant challenges for hemp. The introduction of synthetic fibers and the rise of the pharmaceutical industry saw hemp's natural versatility overshadowed by man-made alternatives. The situation was further exacerbated by the Marihuana Tax Act of 1937 in the United States, which imposed heavy taxes and regulatory burdens on cannabis cultivation, inadvertently affecting hemp due to its association with marijuana. This legislative action, fueled by misinformation and economic interests, marked the beginning of hemp's decline in the Western world.

Despite these setbacks, the late 20th and early 21st centuries have seen a global resurgence of interest in hemp, sparked by a growing awareness of its environmental benefits and potential for sustainable production. Modern research has begun to unlock the plant's ecological advantages, such as its ability to grow with minimal water and pesticides, its role in carbon sequestration, and its potential to replace non-biodegradable materials in products ranging from plastics to concrete. The 2018 Farm Bill in the United States, which legalized hemp cultivation, marked a significant turning point, paving the way for a new era of industrial, nutritional, and therapeutic applications.

Astrology Through the Ages: Tracing the Origins, Evolution, and the Role of Astrology in Agriculture and Herbalism

Astrology's tale is as old as the stars, rooted in humanity's innate desire to find order in the cosmos. Its beginnings can be traced back to the ancient Babylonians, who developed a sophisticated system for predicting celestial events and their earthly impacts. This early form of astrology was deeply entwined with their religious beliefs and daily practices, serving as a guide for everything from farming to governance.

The Greeks, inheriting knowledge from the Babylonians and Egyptians, made significant contributions to astrology, integrating it with their philosophical and scientific inquiries. It was during the Hellenistic period that the zodiac, as we know it today, was fully formed, dividing the sky into twelve signs based on the constellations. This period also saw the birth of horoscopic astrology, which uses the position of celestial bodies at the time of an individual's birth to predict their character and destiny.

In the Middle Ages, astrology flourished in the Islamic world, where scholars translated ancient texts and made new advancements in astronomical observations. Islamic astrologers introduced the use of astrological charts and refined the art of prediction, influencing the Renaissance in Europe, where astrology was embraced by scholars and royalty alike.

Astrology's application in agriculture and herbalism dates back to these ancient times, when planting and harvesting were often conducted according to the lunar calendar and the positions of the planets. This practice, based on the belief in a cosmic connection between the heavens and the earth, aimed to harness celestial energies to ensure bountiful crops and potent herbs. Herbalists attributed plants to specific planets and signs, using this knowledge to enhance the efficacy of remedies and treatments.

Despite the rise of empirical science and the decline of astrology's prominence in the modern era, the 20th century witnessed a resurgence of interest in astrological practices. This revival is not merely a return to tradition but reflects a broader search for meaning and connectivity in an increasingly fragmented world. Today, the principles of astrological agriculture and herbalism are being revisited and integrated into holistic and sustainable practices, offering new ways to understand and interact with the natural world.

Chapter 1 not only recounts the histories of hemp and astrology but also sets the stage for a deeper exploration of their interconnectedness. As we move forward, we will delve into the cosmic rhythms that guide the cultivation of hemp and the ancient wisdom that informs our use of this versatile plant, weaving together the past and present into a tapestry of holistic understanding.

The History of Hemp is extensive, please look into *Marijuana Hater's Guide to Making Billion Dollars from HEMP: The Next Disruptive Industry by Matthew Harmon.*

Get some amazing products from my virtual dispensary here:
https://shift.store/sg1fan23477/retail

Chapter 2: Hemp Unveiled

Botany and Science of Hemp: Discussing Hemp's Classification, Chemical Profiles, Health Benefits, and Therapeutic Applications

Hemp, scientifically known as *Cannabis sativa L.*, is a member of the Cannabaceae family and is one of the oldest crops cultivated by humans. Despite its close genetic relationship to marijuana (*Cannabis sativa* var. *indica*), hemp is distinguished by its chemical composition and lower concentrations of tetrahydrocannabinol (THC), the psychoactive compound found in higher doses in marijuana. Hemp is characterized by its robust growth, capable of reaching up to 4 meters in height, and its ability to thrive in a wide range of climates without the need for excessive pesticides or water, making it an environmentally friendly crop.

The chemical profile of hemp is complex and rich, containing over 100 cannabinoids, with cannabidiol (CBD) being the most prominent due to its significant health benefits without the psychoactive effects of THC. Hemp also contains terpenes, flavonoids, and various nutrients, contributing to its therapeutic potential. Research has highlighted CBD's effectiveness in treating a variety of conditions, including anxiety, chronic pain, epilepsy, and inflammation, positioning hemp as a cornerstone in the emerging field of natural medicine.

Beyond cannabinoids, hemp seeds are a nutritional powerhouse, rich in essential fatty acids like omega-3 and omega-6, proteins, fiber, vitamins, and minerals. This nutritional profile makes hemp seeds and their oil beneficial for heart health, reducing inflammation, and supporting overall well-being.

Hemp's Role in Industry: Examining Hemp's Versatility in Textiles, Construction, Beauty Products, and Beyond

Hemp's industrial applications are as varied as they are innovative, showcasing the plant's unparalleled versatility. Historically, hemp was primarily used in textiles, with its strong fibers being woven into durable fabrics, ropes, and sails. Today, this tradition continues with hemp textiles offering a sustainable alternative to cotton and synthetic fibers, requiring less water and pesticides to produce and providing fabrics with excellent durability, breathability, and antibacterial properties.

In the construction industry, hemp is revolutionizing sustainable building practices through the creation of hempcrete, a lightweight, biodegradable material made from hemp hurds (the inner woody core of the hemp stalk) mixed with lime and water. Hempcrete's natural insulation properties, durability, and carbon-sequestering capabilities make it an ideal material for eco-friendly construction projects.

The beauty and skincare industries have also embraced hemp, with hemp seed oil becoming a coveted ingredient in products ranging from moisturizers and serums to soaps and shampoos. Rich in vitamins and fatty acids, hemp seed oil is lauded for its ability to hydrate, soothe inflammation, and regulate skin oil production, making it suitable for a wide range of skin types and conditions.

Furthermore, hemp's role extends into more innovative sectors, such as bioplastics and biofuels, offering renewable alternatives to petroleum-based products. Hemp bioplastics are biodegradable and possess a strength comparable to conventional plastics, while hemp biofuels present a less polluting energy source, further cementing hemp's status as a plant of the future.

Chapter 2 delves into the botanical essence and scientific revelations of hemp, revealing its classification, unique chemical makeup, and the extensive research underscoring its health benefits and therapeutic applications. Additionally, it showcases hemp's transformative role across various industries, from textiles and construction to beauty products and beyond, highlighting its adaptability and potential as a sustainable resource. As we continue to explore the depth and breadth of hemp's capabilities, it becomes clear that this ancient crop holds keys to addressing contemporary environmental and health challenges, embodying a bridge between the past and a more sustainable future.

Get some amazing products from my virtual dispensary here: https://shift.store/sg1fan23477/retail

Chapter 3: Astrological Principles and Practices

The Foundations of Astrology: Understanding Zodiac Signs, Planets, Elements, and Modalities

Astrology, at its core, is the study of how celestial bodies influence life on Earth. This ancient practice is built upon several foundational components: the zodiac signs, planets, elements, and modalities. Each of these elements plays a crucial role in shaping the astrological profile of an individual or event.

Zodiac Signs: The zodiac is a belt of the heavens within about 8° on either side of the ecliptic, including all apparent positions of the sun, moon, and most familiar planets. It is divided into twelve signs, each covering 30° of celestial longitude, corresponding to the constellations. These signs are Aries, Taurus, Gemini, Cancer, Leo, Virgo, Libra, Scorpio, Sagittarius, Capricorn, Aquarius, and Pisces. Each sign has its characteristics and is associated with specific traits, strengths, and weaknesses. The sun sign, determined by one's birth date, is the most commonly known aspect of astrology, often used as a primary indicator of one's personality.

Planets: In astrology, planets have symbolic meanings, with each governing specific aspects of life and personality. The "personal planets" (Sun, Moon, Mercury, Venus, and Mars) affect individual traits and characteristics, while the "social planets" (Jupiter and Saturn) influence broader societal and generational trends. The "transpersonal planets" (Uranus, Neptune, and Pluto) are associated with transformational forces and generational shifts. Each planet's position in the zodiac at the time of one's birth is said to influence different facets of their life and character.

Elements: The four elements—fire, earth, air, and water—categorize the zodiac signs into four groups, each containing three signs. Fire signs (Aries, Leo, Sagittarius) are known for their passion, energy, and assertiveness. Earth signs (Taurus, Virgo, Capricorn) are practical, grounded, and reliable. Air signs (Gemini, Libra, Aquarius) are intellectual, communicative, and social. Water signs (Cancer, Scorpio, Pisces) are intuitive, emotional, and sensitive. The elemental nature of a sign helps to describe basic personality traits and temperamental dispositions.

Modalities: Modalities, or qualities, further categorize the zodiac signs into three groups: cardinal, fixed, and mutable. Cardinal signs (Aries, Cancer, Libra, Capricorn) initiate change and are leaders. Fixed signs (Taurus, Leo, Scorpio, Aquarius) are stable, determined, and persistent. Mutable signs (Gemini, Virgo, Sagittarius, Pisces) are adaptable and flexible, capable of change and transformation. The modality of a sign reveals its approach to life and change.

The Astrological Chart: Diving into Houses, Aspects, and the Significance of Transits and Natal Charts

The astrological chart, or birth chart, is a snapshot of the heavens at the moment of one's birth, providing a cosmic roadmap to one's personality, life events, and potential. This chart is divided into twelve segments, known as houses, each representing different areas of life, such as identity, relationships, career, and aspirations. The placement of planets within these houses, and their relationships to one another, are critically analyzed in astrology.

Houses: Each house corresponds to various aspects of life, with the first house (or Ascendant) representing the self and personal identity, and the other houses moving through different spheres such as possessions, communication, home and family, creativity and pleasure, work and health, partnerships, transformations, philosophy and travel, career and reputation, community and friendships, and finally, the subconscious and spirituality. The positioning of planets within these houses influences how the energies of the planets manifest in different areas of one's life.

Aspects: Aspects are angles formed by the planets in relation to each other within the birth chart, indicating how the planets interact and influence each other. Major aspects include conjunctions (aligned or in the same sign), oppositions (across the zodiac), squares (90° apart), trines (120° apart), and sextiles (60° apart). These relationships can be harmonious or challenging, affecting the flow of energy in the chart and highlighting areas of potential growth, conflict, or ease.

Transits and Natal Charts: A natal chart remains a constant, a celestial imprint of the moment of birth. Transits, however, refer to the movement of the planets in the sky at any given time after birth and their interaction with the natal chart. Transits can activate different parts of the natal chart, signifying times of challenge, opportunity, or transformation. Understanding transits is crucial for predictive astrology, offering insights into the timing of significant life events and personal developments. These celestial movements provide a dynamic layer to the static natal chart, illustrating how the continuous motion of the planets influences our evolving life story.

Transits are particularly important for understanding the phases of growth, challenge, and reevaluation in one's life. For example, the return of Saturn, occurring approximately every 29.5 years, is often associated with major life milestones, trials, and maturation. Similarly, the faster-moving planets like Mercury, Venus, and Mars create shorter cycles that can highlight periods of communication changes, relationship developments, and shifts in energy and ambition.

The interaction between transiting planets and those in the natal chart can illuminate potential areas of change. A transit might make an exact aspect to a natal planet, activating its energies in a way that can be felt more directly in the individual's life. These periods can be seen as windows of opportunity for growth, learning, and adjustment, emphasizing the importance of free will and personal choice in navigating these cosmic influences.

Understanding the significance of transits and how they interact with a natal chart is akin to reading a cosmic weather report. Just as one might dress appropriately for the weather forecast, knowing one's astrological forecast can prepare them for the emotional, psychological, and circumstantial climates they may encounter. This awareness allows individuals to work with the energies at play, harnessing favorable transits for advancement and navigating challenging aspects with awareness and grace.

Moreover, the study of transits in relation to the natal chart underscores the notion that astrology is not deterministic but rather a tool for self-awareness and growth. It presents a nuanced framework for understanding the ebbs and flows of life's cycles, offering guidance on how to align one's actions with the cosmic tides. By paying attention to these celestial influences, one can gain deeper insights into their personal evolution, unlocking potentials and navigating life's challenges with greater ease.

In summary, the natal chart provides a foundational blueprint of an individual's potentials and challenges, while transits reveal the timing and nature of experiences that activate and test these aspects of the self. Together, they form a comprehensive astrological perspective, offering a profound and dynamic understanding of the individual's journey through life. As we explore astrology's principles and practices, we gain not only knowledge of the cosmos but also a deeper understanding of ourselves and our place within the universe.

Get some amazing products from my virtual dispensary here: https://shift.store/sg1fan23477/retail

Chapter 4: Synchronizing Hemp with Astrology

Astrological Profiles of Hemp: Identifying Hemp's Ruling Planets, Optimal Planting and Harvesting Times, and Growth Conditions

The intersection of astrology and horticulture offers a unique lens through which we can view the cultivation and use of hemp. By understanding hemp's astrological profile, we can align our agricultural practices with celestial rhythms, optimizing the plant's vitality, yield, and therapeutic qualities.

Hemp's Ruling Planets: Traditionally, each plant is believed to fall under the dominion of one or more celestial bodies, which influence its growth, characteristics, and healing properties. Hemp is primarily associated with Saturn, reflecting the planet's attributes of endurance, resilience, and utility. Saturn's influence imbues hemp with its hardy nature, allowing it to thrive in various conditions and lending it the strength for which its fibers are renowned. Additionally, Mercury's association with hemp highlights the plant's versatility and its capacity to serve multiple purposes, from textiles to medicine.

Optimal Planting and Harvesting Times: Aligning hemp cultivation with the lunar cycle and planetary positions can enhance the plant's growth and potency. Planting seeds during the waxing moon, when lunar gravity pulls water upward, can improve seed germination and root growth. Harvesting during the waning moon, meanwhile, is believed to concentrate the plant's energies and chemical compounds, enhancing its medicinal properties.

Specific astrological events, such as the moon's transit through fertile, earth-sign constellations (Taurus, Virgo, Capricorn), offer favorable conditions for planting. Conversely, harvesting is ideally conducted when the moon is in a fixed sign (Taurus, Leo, Scorpio, Aquarius), which is thought to stabilize and preserve the plant's qualities.

Growth Conditions: Beyond timing, the astrological profile of hemp suggests a preference for well-drained soil and a balance between sunlight and shade, reflecting Saturn's association with structure and Mercury's with adaptability. The plant's resilience is enhanced when grown in conditions that honor these planetary influences, promoting robust health and minimizing the need for chemical interventions.

Hemp Use and Your Astrological Blueprint: Tailoring Hemp Product Selection and Use to Individual Astrological Profiles

Astrology can also guide the personalized use of hemp, from choosing the right type of product to determining the most auspicious times for its use. By considering one's astrological blueprint—namely, the sun, moon, and rising signs—individuals can select hemp products that resonate with their specific energetic needs and health objectives.

Tailoring to Sun Signs: The sun sign, indicating one's core identity and vitality, can guide the selection of hemp products for overall wellness. Fire signs (Aries, Leo, Sagittarius) may benefit from hemp-based products that support energy and metabolism, while earth signs (Taurus, Virgo, Capricorn) might prefer products that enhance physical strength and grounding. Air signs (Gemini, Libra, Aquarius) could find hemp products that aid communication and mental clarity most beneficial, whereas water signs (Cancer, Scorpio, Pisces) might seek out hemp's calming and nurturing properties.

Aligning with Moon Signs: The moon sign, reflecting emotional and nurturing needs, can inform the use of hemp for emotional balance and comfort. Products rich in CBD may be particularly soothing for those with moon signs in water or fire, helping to calm emotional turbulence or temper intensity. For moon signs in earth or air, hemp products might best support practical emotional regulation and mental wellness.

Considering Rising Signs: The rising sign, or ascendant, representing one's approach to life and first impressions, can influence the choice of hemp products for external use, such as skincare or apparel. For instance, rising signs in earth might gravitate towards hemp-based textiles for their durability and comfort, while those with air rising signs may appreciate hemp's breathability and lightness.

Astrological Timing: Beyond selection, astrology can guide the timing of hemp use for health and wellness rituals. Initiating a CBD regimen during a new moon, for example, can symbolize and support new beginnings in one's health journey. Conversely, using hemp for detoxification or release might be most potent during the full moon, aligning with themes of culmination and release.

Chapter 4 unveils the profound connection between hemp and astrology, offering insights into how celestial influences can optimize the cultivation, harvest, and personal use of hemp. By synchronizing our practices with the cosmos, we not only enhance the physical and therapeutic qualities of hemp but also deepen our connection to the natural world, embodying a holistic approach to wellness that honors the ancient wisdom of both the earth and the stars.

**Get some amazing products from my virtual dispensary here:
https://shift.store/sg1fan23477/retail**

Chapter 5: From Seed to Spirit: Astrological Applications in Hemp Cultivation and use.

Cultivating Hemp Under Celestial Guidance: Using Lunar and Planetary Timings for Planting, Growth, and Pest Control

The cultivation of hemp, like many agricultural practices, can benefit significantly from aligning with celestial cycles. Ancient wisdom and modern biodynamic farming both emphasize the importance of planting and tending to crops in harmony with the moon's phases and planetary positions. This section delves into how these cosmic timings can influence hemp cultivation, enhancing growth and yield, and even assisting in natural pest control.

Lunar Phases and Planting: The lunar cycle, with its waxing and waning phases, plays a pivotal role in the optimal timing for planting hemp. The waxing phase, from the new moon to the full moon, is believed to encourage growth in above-ground biomass. This period is ideal for sowing hemp seeds as the increasing moonlight is thought to stimulate leaf and stem development. Conversely, the waning phase is more conducive to root growth. For hemp, primarily cultivated for its stems and leaves, focusing on the waxing phase can capitalize on its growth potential.

Planetary Influences: Beyond the moon, the positions of other planets also contribute to the energetic environment for plant growth. Jupiter, the planet of expansion and growth, is particularly beneficial for planting endeavors. Aligning hemp planting with Jupiter's favorable aspects, such as trines or conjunctions with the sun or moon, can potentially enhance the plant's development and yield. Mars, associated with energy and action, can influence pest resistance and plant vitality when favorably positioned.

Biodynamic Preparations and Pest Control: Biodynamic agriculture, which applies astrological principles to farming, uses special preparations to enrich the soil and deter pests, integrating cosmic rhythms into the cultivation process. By observing the moon's passage through the zodiac, farmers can apply these preparations at times most conducive to absorption by the plants and soil. For instance, applying nettle tea during a Scorpio moon, a sign associated with transformation and deep healing, may enhance the plant's natural resistance to pests and diseases.

Crafting Personalized Hemp Products: Recipes and Instructions for Creating Hemp-Infused Products Aligned with Astrological Insights

The creation of hemp-infused products can also benefit from astrological insights, allowing for the crafting of personalized remedies and enhancements that resonate with individual needs and cosmic energies. This section explores how to harness these energies through tailored recipes and preparations.

Hemp Oil Infusions: Creating a hemp oil infusion during a specific lunar phase or under particular planetary alignments can imbue the oil with those celestial qualities. For example, infusing hemp oil with calming herbs like lavender or chamomile during a full moon in Pisces can enhance its soothing effects, ideal for stress relief and relaxation. The full moon's energy amplifies the infusion's potency, while Pisces' influence deepens the emotional and spiritual resonance of the blend.

Hemp-Based Edibles: The preparation of hemp edibles can also align with astrological timings for enhanced effect. Baking hemp-infused goods when the moon is in Taurus, a sign that rules over tastes and comfort, can augment the enjoyment and satisfaction derived from them. Additionally, considering Mars' position can optimize the edibles for energy or action, making them perfect for activities requiring stamina and vitality.

Topical Hemp Products: For hemp-based creams, lotions, and balms, crafting these during specific zodiac sign transits can target different skin concerns. Creating a hemp moisturizer while the moon is in Virgo, a sign associated with health and purification, can be particularly effective for skin healing and detoxification. Incorporating essential oils that correspond with the moon's sign can further enhance the product's therapeutic properties.

Through the alignment of hemp cultivation and product creation with celestial guidance, individuals can tap into the ancient wisdom that links the cosmos with the natural world. This harmonization not only enriches the physical benefits of hemp but also imbues these practices and products with deeper spiritual and energetic qualities, creating a truly holistic approach to wellness that spans from seed to spirit.

You will find many unique things that you can do with Hemp, Today.

Check out my Virtual Dispensary for some amazing edibles, drinks Pre-Rolls and more: https://shift.store/sg1fan23477/retail

Chapter Six: The Heavenly Hemp Lifestyle.

The harmonious blend of hemp and astrology extends beyond the realms of cultivation and crafting, permeating the very essence of daily life, dietary practices, beauty regimens, and even the spaces we inhabit. This chapter explores how to weave these elements into a holistic lifestyle, aligning with cosmic energies for enhanced well-being, comfort, and spiritual connectivity.

Integrating Hemp and Astrology into Daily Life

Daily Routines and Astrological Timing: Begin each day by aligning your activities with the moon's phase and the zodiac sign it's currently traversing. For example, mornings when the moon is in an energetic sign like Aries or Leo are perfect for incorporating hemp-based protein smoothies or bars to fuel your day with vitality. Conversely, during a moon in water signs like Cancer or Pisces, a calming hemp tea might be more appropriate to nurture emotional well-being and intuition.

Dietary Practices with Cosmic Consideration: Tailor your diet to the astrological climate by including hemp in meals that correspond with the current moon sign. When the moon is in earth signs (Taurus, Virgo, Capricorn), focus on grounding and nourishing meals, adding hemp seeds to salads or soups. Air sign moons (Gemini, Libra, Aquarius) call for lighter, brain-boosting meals, such as hemp seed pesto or smoothies that support communication and social connections.

Beauty Regimens Aligned with the Stars: Personalize your beauty and self-care practices by creating a hemp-based skincare routine that resonates with the astrological energies. During a Venus transit, enhance your beauty regimen with hemp oil serums or masks to tap into Venus's association with love and beauty. A full moon in earthy Virgo is the ideal time for a detoxifying hemp clay mask, focusing on purification and health.

Astrologically Inspired Hemp Living Spaces

Hemp Materials in Home Design: Incorporate hemp textiles and materials into your living environment to create a space that's not only eco-friendly but also vibrationally aligned with celestial energies. Use hemp curtains, rugs, and upholstery in colors and patterns that resonate with your personal astrology to enhance specific areas of your life. For instance, a bedroom adorned with soft blue hemp linens can invite tranquil, healing energies, especially beneficial when Neptune is active in your chart, promoting rest and dreams.

Seasonal Decorations and Energy Flow: Align your home's energy with the seasons and astrological cycles by integrating hemp-based decorations that reflect the current zodiac season. During Aries season, bright red hemp cushions can invigorate your living space with energy and initiative. In contrast, Cancer season might see the addition of cozy, white hemp throws to nurture and comfort. Utilize hemp decorations not only for their aesthetic but for their ability to harmonize and attract positive cosmic vibrations.

Feng Shui and Astrological Elements: Apply principles of Feng Shui, considering your astrological element to arrange your living spaces in a way that promotes balance and flow. For a water sign, incorporating a small hemp fabric water element in the north of your home can enhance personal growth and introspection. Fire signs might place a hemp candle in the south for passion and recognition. Through these mindful placements, your environment becomes a reflection of the cosmic balance, supporting your journey both spiritually and materially.

The integration of hemp and astrology into daily life and living spaces offers a profound way to live in harmony with the natural and cosmic worlds. By consciously choosing to align our habits, diets, beauty practices, and environments with the celestial energies, we invite balance, health, and spiritual well-being into our lives, embodying the heavenly hemp lifestyle.

You will find many great things in my Virtual Dispensary that can give the ultimate 'Heavenly Hemp Lifestyle" from many products on the site: https://shift.store/sg1fan23477/retail

Conclusion: Weaving Together the Cosmic and the Earthly.

As we reach the conclusion of our journey through the realms of hemp and astrology, it becomes evident that the tapestry of existence is woven with threads that connect the cosmic to the earthly, the celestial to the botanical, and the individual to the collective. This exploration has revealed the profound interconnections between the movements of celestial bodies and the growth of plants on Earth, and how these relationships can be harnessed to enhance personal well-being, spiritual growth, and environmental sustainability.

Reflections on the Deep Connection Between the Cosmos, Plants, and Personal Well-Being

The journey through the pages of this book has illuminated the ancient wisdom that recognizes the universe as a coherent, interconnected system where the macrocosm of the cosmos is reflected in the microcosm of earthly life. This cosmic-earthly connection is vividly embodied in the plant of hemp—a plant that has served humanity in myriad ways for thousands of years, and whose growth and utility are influenced by celestial rhythms and cycles.

Astrology offers a language and a framework through which we can understand and interact with these cosmic influences. By aligning our practices of cultivating, utilizing, and integrating hemp into our lives with the movements of the planets and the phases of the moon, we not only optimize the physical benefits that hemp has to offer but also open ourselves to deeper spiritual and energetic insights. This alignment encourages a holistic approach to well-being that encompasses physical health, emotional balance, and spiritual fulfillment.

Encouragement for Readers to Explore Their Own Relationship with Hemp and Astrology, and to Contribute to a Community of Like-Minded Individuals

This book is an invitation to embark on a personal exploration of the connections between hemp, astrology, and yourself. It is an encouragement to observe, experiment, and experience how the celestial influences interact with your life and well-being, and how integrating hemp into this dynamic can amplify your alignment with the natural and cosmic forces.

You are invited to delve deeper into the practices and insights shared within these pages, to personalize them according to your unique astrological blueprint and life circumstances. Whether it's by choosing the right time to plant hemp seeds, creating personalized hemp-infused products, or integrating hemp into your diet and lifestyle in harmony with the stars, there are endless possibilities for enriching your life with the wisdom of the cosmos and the earth.

Moreover, this journey is not one that needs to be undertaken alone. There exists a vibrant, growing community of like-minded individuals who share a passion for understanding and living in harmony with the cosmic and earthly realms. By connecting with this community—whether through social media, forums, workshops, or local groups—you can share experiences, gain insights, and contribute to a collective pool of knowledge that enriches everyone involved.

As we weave together the cosmic and the earthly in our lives, we contribute to a larger pattern of consciousness and healing that extends beyond our individual existence. This book, therefore, is not just a conclusion but a beginning—a point of departure for an ongoing journey of discovery, growth, and connection. May your exploration of hemp and astrology bring you closer to the harmony of the cosmos, deepen your connection with the Earth, and illuminate your path to well-being.

Get some amazing products from my virtual dispensary here: https://shift.store/sg1fan23477/retail

1. Comprehensive guide to Hemp Products and their uses

.

Hemp, a versatile and sustainable crop, offers a wide array of products that cater to different aspects of our daily lives, from health and nutrition to sustainable living and beyond. This guide provides an extensive overview of hemp products, highlighting their applications and benefits, thereby showcasing hemp's incredible adaptability and potential to contribute to a more sustainable and health-conscious world.

Hemp Foods and Nutritional Products

1. **Hemp Seeds**: Packed with protein, essential fatty acids, vitamins, and minerals, hemp seeds are a nutritional powerhouse. They can be eaten raw, ground into hemp meal, sprouted, or made into dried sprout powder. Hemp seeds can also be pressed into oil, which is used in cooking, salad dressings, and dips.
2. **Hemp Seed Oil**: Extracted from the seeds of the hemp plant, this oil is high in omega-3 and omega-6 fatty acids, making it an excellent dietary supplement for heart health and skin vitality. It's also used as a base for CBD products.
3. **Hemp Protein Powder**: A by-product of pressing hemp seed oil, this powder is an ideal protein supplement, offering a complete amino acid profile which is rare in plant-based proteins. It's perfect for smoothies, baking, or as a meal replacement.
4. **Hemp Milk**: Made from blended hemp seeds and water, hemp milk is a nutritious, dairy-free alternative, rich in plant-based proteins and healthy fats.

Hemp Textiles and Clothing

1. **Hemp Fabric**: Known for its durability, hemp fabric is used in making apparel, bags, shoes, and accessories. It's breathable, anti-

bacterial, and biodegradable, making it an eco-friendly choice for clothing.

2. **Hemp Shoes and Accessories**: Utilizing hemp fabric, these products offer an environmentally sustainable option for fashion-conscious consumers. They're known for their strength and durability.

Hemp Body Care and Beauty Products

1. **Hemp-Based Soaps and Lotions**: Due to hemp oil's moisturizing and skin beneficial properties, it's a common ingredient in soaps, lotions, and balms. These products help in restoring the skin's barrier, preventing dryness, and promoting skin health.

2. **Hemp CBD Products**: CBD, derived from hemp, is used in a variety of skincare and therapeutic products, including creams, balms, tinctures, and capsules. CBD is celebrated for its potential to relieve pain, reduce anxiety, and support overall wellness.

Industrial Hemp Products

1. **Hempcrete**: A bio-composite material used in construction, hempcrete is made from the woody inner fibers of the hemp stalk mixed with lime and water. It's lightweight, breathable, and offers excellent insulation properties.

2. **Hemp Plastics**: Hemp fibers can be used to create biodegradable plastics, offering a sustainable alternative to petroleum-based plastics. These are used in a variety of products, including packaging, car parts, and more.

3. **Hemp Paper**: Sustainable and eco-friendly, hemp paper is made from hemp pulp. It requires fewer chemicals for processing than traditional wood paper, making it a greener alternative.

Hemp in Gardening and Agriculture

1. **Hemp Mulch and Compost**: Hemp stalks and fibers can be used as mulch and compost, enriching the soil and retaining moisture without the use of chemical fertilizers.
2. **Hemp Animal Bedding**: Highly absorbent and low in dust, hemp bedding is ideal for horses, chickens, and small animals. It's biodegradable and compostable, reducing waste and promoting animal health.

This comprehensive guide to hemp products showcases the plant's versatility and its potential to contribute positively to various sectors, including nutrition, fashion, beauty, construction, and more. By incorporating hemp into our daily lives, we take a step towards more sustainable living practices, benefiting not only our health but also the environment.

There are many items that you can use in my Virtual Dispensary: https://shift.store/sg1fan23477/retail

-

-

-

-

-

-

-

-

-

-

-

-

-
-
-
-
-
-
-

Astrological Calendar for Hemp Cultivation
Spring Equinox: Aries Season (March 20 - April 19)

- **New Beginnings and Planting**: The Spring Equinox marks the start of the astrological year and Aries season, making it an auspicious time to begin new ventures, including the planting of hemp seeds. Aries is a cardinal fire sign, symbolizing initiation and action. Planting during this time can imbue your crop with the energetic qualities of growth and vitality.

Taurus Season (April 20 - May 20)

- **Soil Preparation and Planting Continuation**: Taurus, a fixed earth sign, emphasizes stability, nourishment, and growth. This period is ideal for preparing the soil, enriching it with nutrients, and continuing the planting process. Taurus's grounding energy supports root development.

Gemini Season (May 21 - June 20)

- **Pollination and Communication**: With Gemini, a mutable air sign, focus shifts to pollination processes and the health of the aerial parts of the plant. This is a time for ensuring open lines of communication in your gardening community, sharing tips, and learning about pest control and plant care.

Summer Solstice: Cancer Season (June 21 - July 22)

- **Watering and Nurturing**: The Summer Solstice ushers in Cancer season, a cardinal water sign, highlighting the importance of water and nourishment for your hemp crop. Emphasize consistent watering schedules and protect your plants from the intense midsummer sun.

Leo Season (July 23 - August 22)

- **Strength and Vitality**: Leo, a fixed fire sign, is associated with strength, courage, and vitality. During this period, focus on supporting the strong growth of your hemp plants. This might include practices that encourage robust stem and leaf development.

Virgo Season (August 23 - September 22)

- **Health and Routine**: Virgo, a mutable earth sign, brings attention to the health of the crop, encouraging a routine check for pests and diseases. It's also a good time to consider the practical aspects of your cultivation, such as organization and efficiency.

Fall Equinox: Libra Season (September 23 - October 22)

- **Harvesting and Balance**: The Fall Equinox and Libra season, a cardinal air sign, represent balance and harmony, making it an optimal time to begin harvesting your hemp crop. Libra's energy supports equitable and balanced harvesting practices, ensuring that each plant is given attention.

Scorpio Season (October 23 - November 21)

- **Transformation and Processing**: Scorpio, a fixed water sign, is associated with transformation. This period is suitable for processing the harvested hemp, such as drying and curing, where transformation from raw to finished product takes place.

Sagittarius Season (November 22 - December 21)

- **Expansion and Planning for the Next Cycle**: Sagittarius, a mutable fire sign, encourages looking ahead and planning for the future. This is a time to reflect on the cultivation cycle and plan for the next year, considering expansion and exploration of new cultivation techniques.

Winter Solstice: Capricorn Season (December 22 - January 19)

- **Rest and Reflection**: The Winter Solstice marks Capricorn season, a cardinal earth sign that emphasizes structure, discipline, and reflection. This is a period for rest and contemplation, analyzing the successes and lessons of the past cultivation cycle, and setting goals for the future.

Aquarius Season (January 20 - February 18) and Pisces Season (February 19 - March 20)

- **Innovation and Preparation**: These two seasons, representing a fixed air sign and a mutable water sign, respectively, are times for innovative thinking and spiritual preparation for the cycle to begin anew. Aquarius encourages experimental approaches to cultivation, while Pisces focuses on connecting with the spiritual aspect of agriculture.

This astrological calendar provides a rhythm to hemp cultivation that aligns with the energies of the zodiac, offering a holistic approach to farming that considers both the earth and the cosmos. By tuning into these cycles, growers can work in harmony with nature, potentially enhancing the vitality and yield of their hemp crops.

Get some amazing products from my virtual dispensary here: https://shift.store/sg1fan23477/retail

-
-
-
-
-
-
-
-
-
-
-
-
-
-
-
-
-
-
-
-
-

Glossary of Astrological and Hemp Terms

This glossary is designed to provide clear definitions for key terms related to astrology and hemp that have been used throughout the book. Understanding these terms will enhance comprehension of the concepts presented and facilitate a deeper exploration of the subjects.

Astrological Terms

1. **Ascendant (Rising Sign)**: The zodiac sign that was rising on the eastern horizon at the time of one's birth. It represents one's outward demeanor and how others perceive them.
2. **Aspect**: The angular relationship between two planets in a horoscope, which may be harmonious or challenging. Aspects influence how the energies of the planets interact with each other.
3. **Cardinal Signs (Aries, Cancer, Libra, Capricorn)**: Signs that initiate the seasons. They are associated with new beginnings, leadership, and action.
4. **Fixed Signs (Taurus, Leo, Scorpio, Aquarius)**: Signs that fall in the middle of the seasons. They are associated with stability, determination, and persistence.
5. **Mutable Signs (Gemini, Virgo, Sagittarius, Pisces)**: Signs that conclude the seasons. They are associated with adaptability, flexibility, and change.
6. **Natal Chart (Birth Chart)**: A map of where all the planets were in their journey around the Sun, from our vantage point on earth, at the exact moment of one's birth.
7. **Planets**: In astrology, planets represent different components of our psyche and life areas (e.g., Sun represents ego and identity, Moon represents emotions and inner self).

8. **Transit**: The movement of planets in the sky post-birth and their interactions with the natal chart's positions, symbolizing external events and internal changes.

9. **Trine**: An aspect formed when two planets are approximately 120 degrees apart. It is considered the most harmonious aspect, bringing ease and flow.

10. **Zodiac**: The belt of the heavens divided into twelve equal parts, each named after the constellation that originally occupied the segment. It forms the basis of astrological practice.

Hemp Terms

1. **Cannabidiol (CBD)**: A compound found in cannabis and hemp plants known for its health benefits, including reducing anxiety, relieving pain, and improving sleep, without psychoactive effects.
2. **Cannabinoids**: Chemical compounds found in the cannabis plant. Over 100 cannabinoids have been identified, including THC and CBD, each with different effects on the body's endocannabinoid system.
3. **Hempcrete**: A sustainable construction material made from the woody core of the hemp plant mixed with lime and water. It is lightweight, breathable, and has excellent insulation properties.
4. **Hemp Fiber**: The fiber from the stalk of the hemp plant, used historically for ropes, textiles, and paper due to its durability and strength.
5. **Hemp Seed Oil**: Oil extracted from the seeds of the hemp plant, rich in omega fatty acids, vitamins, and minerals. It is used in cooking, cosmetics, and as a dietary supplement.
6. **Hemp Seeds**: The seeds of the hemp plant, considered a superfood due to their high content of proteins, essential fatty acids, and nutrients.
7. **Tetrahydrocannabinol (THC)**: The principal psychoactive constituent of cannabis. Hemp contains THC in very low concentrations, not sufficient to produce a psychoactive effect.
8. **Industrial Hemp**: Varieties of the Cannabis sativa plant species that are grown specifically for industrial uses of its derived products. It has low levels of THC and high levels of CBD.

Understanding these terms provides a solid foundation for navigating the interconnected worlds of astrology and hemp. Whether you're delving into personal growth, exploring sustainable living practices, or seeking to harmonize with the cosmic rhythms, this glossary serves as a valuable reference point on your journey.

Get some amazing products from my virtual dispensary here: https://shift.store/sg1fan23477/retail

Resources for Further Examination

For those captivated by the intersection of hemp and astrology and eager to deepen their understanding, the journey does not end with the closing of this book. A wealth of resources exists to expand your knowledge, connect with like-minded individuals, and explore the multifaceted relationship between the cosmos and cannabis cultivation. Below is a curated list of books, websites, and communities designed to guide you further on this enlightening path.

Books

1. **"The Secret Life of Plants" by Peter Tompkins and Christopher Bird**: This classic explores the intricate relationship between plants and the unseen world, including the influence of cosmic forces on plant life. It provides a foundational understanding of how living organisms interact with the environment, including celestial influences.

2. **"Hemp for Victory: A Global Warming Solution" by Richard Rose and Steven Hager**: Focusing on the environmental and sustainable aspects of hemp, this book delves into how hemp cultivation can contribute to solving global warming. It's a must-read for those interested in the ecological impact of hemp.

3. **"Astrology for the Soul" by Jan Spiller**: An insightful book that offers a deep dive into the nodes of the moon, providing an astrological perspective on the soul's purpose. This book helps readers understand the deeper spiritual implications of their astrological placements.

4. **"The Emperor Wears No Clothes" by Jack Herer**: A comprehensive book on hemp, its history, uses, and the politics that have surrounded its cultivation. Herer's work is pivotal

for understanding the socio-economic barriers to hemp and its potential as a sustainable resource.

5. **"Astrological Gardening" by Louise Riotte**: Specifically focusing on the use of astrology in gardening, this book guides readers through the best times to plant, tend, and harvest based on the moon's phases and astrological signs. It's particularly relevant for those interested in biodynamic farming principles.

Websites

1. **Project CBD (projectcbd.org)**: A non-profit dedicated to promoting and publicizing research into the medical uses of CBD and other components of the cannabis plant. This site is an excellent resource for those looking to understand the therapeutic aspects of hemp.

2. **The Astrology Podcast (theastrologypodcast.com)**: Offers a wealth of knowledge on various astrological topics, including traditional and modern techniques, historical insights, and current astrological events.

3. **Hemp Industries Association (thehia.org)**: A non-profit trade association representing hemp companies, researchers, and supporters. The HIA provides resources on hemp legislation, cultivation, and market trends.

4. **Astrodienst (astro.com)**: A comprehensive site for creating personal astrological charts and reports. It offers tools for both beginners and advanced students of astrology, including free chart calculations and detailed interpretations.

Communities

1. **Reddit - r/Astrology and r/Hemp**: These subreddits offer spaces for discussion and information exchange on astrology and hemp, respectively. Members share insights, ask questions, and connect over shared interests.

2. **The Biodynamic Association (biodynamics.com)**: Though not exclusively focused on hemp, this community integrates astrological principles in farming. It offers workshops, conferences, and certification programs in biodynamic agriculture.

3. **United Astrology Conference (uacastrology.com)**: Considered one of the largest gatherings of astrologers in the world, the UAC offers workshops, lectures, and opportunities to network with professional astrologers.

By exploring these resources, readers can continue to expand their knowledge of hemp and astrology, integrating these ancient practices into a modern context. Whether through reading, online exploration, or community engagement, the journey into the cosmic and earthly realms of hemp cultivation offers endless opportunities for growth, learning, and connection.

Get some amazing products from my virtual dispensary here: https://shift.store/sg1fan23477/retail

References:

Scientific Research and Hemp Studies

1. "The Pharmacological Potential of Cannabidiol" by J. Borrelli, E. Pagano, M. Romano, et al. in the *Journal of Pharmacology & Experimental Therapeutics*, 2017. This study offers insight into the therapeutic benefits of CBD, exploring its anti-inflammatory, analgesic, and anxiolytic properties.
2. "Industrial Hemp in North America: Production, Politics, and Potential" by Jerome H. Cherney and Ernest Small in *Agronomy*, 2016. This paper provides a comprehensive overview of hemp's industrial applications, its environmental benefits, and the legal challenges it has faced.

Historical Documents and Ethnobotanical Studies

1. "Hemp: American History Revisited" by Robert Deitch. This book delves into the historical significance of hemp in the United States, detailing its impact on economic and social development.
2. "The Emperor Wears No Clothes" by Jack Herer. A seminal work on the history of hemp and cannabis prohibition, exploring the socio-political reasons behind the criminalization of these plants.

Astrological Texts and Foundations

1. **"Tetrabiblos" by Claudius Ptolemy.** Often considered the foundational text of Western astrology, this work outlines the philosophical underpinnings of astrological practice in the 2nd century.
2. **"The Only Astrology Book You'll Ever Need" by Joanna Martine Woolfolk.** A comprehensive guide that covers the basics of astrology, including interpretations of planets, signs, and houses, and how to construct a personal horoscope.

Contemporary Analyses and Guides

1. **"Astrology for the Soul" by Jan Spiller.** This book offers a modern take on astrology, focusing on the nodes of the Moon and their significance in personal growth and life purpose.
2. **"The Secret Teachings of Plants: The Intelligence of the Heart in the Direct Perception of Nature" by Stephen Harrod Buhner.** This book explores the idea that plants have much to teach us, not only about our biological and ecological interconnections but also about the nature of consciousness and spirituality.

Environmental Science and Sustainable Agriculture

1. **"Sustainable Agriculture and New Biotechnologies" edited by Nazimi Açıkgöz.** This collection examines the role of new biotechnologies in promoting sustainable agricultural practices, with a focus on genetically modified organisms but also relevant for understanding the broader context in which hemp cultivation might fit.

Legal and Policy Analyses

1. "The Legalization of Marijuana in Colorado: The Impact" by the Rocky Mountain High-Intensity Drug Trafficking Area. A report that provides a comprehensive analysis of the consequences of marijuana and hemp legalization in Colorado, touching upon legal, social, and economic impacts.

By referencing these diverse sources, the book aims to provide a well-rounded perspective on the subjects of hemp and astrology. This compilation not only underscores the rigor and depth of research that underpin the discussion but also serves as a valuable resource for readers seeking to explore these topics further.

<u>Message from the Author:</u>

I hope you enjoyed this book, I love astrology and knew there was not a book such as this out on the shelf. I love metaphysical items as well. Please check out my other books:

-Life of Government Benefits

-My life of Hell

-My life with Hydrocephalus

-Red Sky

-World Domination:Woman's rule

-World Domination:Woman's Rule 2: The War

-Life and Banishment of Apophis: book 1

-The Kidney Friendly Diet

-The Ultimate Hemp Cookbook

-Creating a Dispensary(legally)

-Cleanliness throughout life: the importance of showering from childhood to adulthood,

-Strong Roots: The Risks of Overcoddling children

-Hemp Horoscopes: Cosmic Insights and Earthly Healing

- Celestial Hemp Navigating the Zodiac: Through the Green Cosmos

-Astrological Hemp: Aligning The Stars with Earth's Ancient Herb

-The Astrological Guide to Hemp: Stars, Signs, and Sacred Leaves

-Green Growth: Innovative Marketing Strategies for your Hemp Products and Dispensary

-Cosmic Cannabis

-Astrological Munchies

Check out my Virtual dispensary for all your hemp needs: https://shift.store/sg1fan23477/retail

If you want solar for your home go here: https://www.harbor-solar.live/apophisenterprises/

Instagrams: @apophis_enterprises,   @hempkingdom2024, @apophisbookemporium, @apophisfashion, @apophisscardshop

Twitter: @apophisenterpr1, Tiktok:@apophisenterprise

Youtube: @sg1fan23477Top of Form

Podcast: Apophis Chat Zone: https://open.spotify.com/show/5zXbrCLEV2xzCp8ybrfHsk?si=fb4d4fdbdce44dec

Newsletter: https://apophiss-newsletter-27c897.beehiiv.com/

www.ingramcontent.com/pod-product-compliance
Lightning Source LLC
Chambersburg PA
CBHW051403150726
48000CB00003B/1309